Hartsough

Table of Contents

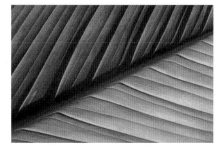

Learning With Nature Idea Book
Copyright © 2007, Reprinted 2008 by the Arbor Day Foundation. All rights reserved.
For information on how to reproduce portions of this book write:
Permissions: The Arbor Day Foundation 211 N. 12th Street Lincoln, NE 68508
ISBN: 978-0-9634657-0-2

RECYCLED PAPER
RECYCLABLE

PRINTED WITH
SOY INK

Why Learning With Nature is Important

"Early experiences with the natural world have been positively linked to the sense of wonder. This way of knowing, if recognized and honored, can serve as a life-long source of joy and enrichment, as well as an impetus or motivation, for further learning."

Ruth A. Wilson, "The Wonders of Nature: Honoring Children's Ways of Knowing"

This book is for anyone wishing to create or re-create outdoor spaces that nurture children's sense of wonder and encourage rich learning. The field-tested guiding principles developed by the Dimensions Educational Research Foundation can be applied in many settings, from early childhood education programs to elementary schools to public playgrounds. The way the principles are implemented will vary greatly, since each organization will bring its unique approach to this undertaking.

The ideas in this book are based on research and field-testing conducted by the Dimensions Foundation in various settings serving children from ages six weeks to 10 years. Dimensions' cadre of teacher-researchers, researchers and consultants from fields such as architecture, landscape architecture, neuropsychology, movement and music, art, mathematics, and science education, have identified profound benefits for children who spend time interacting with nature on a daily basis. The photographs we use illustrate how these field-tested ideas can work for children in urban and rural settings, in cold and warm climates, and in public and private spaces.

Dimensions' research has shown the value of comprehensive nature education for young children that goes beyond simply having well-designed outdoor spaces. Children benefit most in programs that have educators who are knowledgeable about how to use these spaces as an integral part of daily learning, and families who understand and support the need for children to connect with the natural world.

The Dimensions Foundation works in partnership with The National Arbor Day Foundation to develop resources for educators and families to support this important learning. The Arbor Day Foundation believes that if there is to be a new generation of environmental stewards, connecting with nature must once again become an important part of children's daily experiences.

"If a child is to keep alive his inborn sense of wonder, he needs the companionship of at least one adult who can share it, rediscovering the joy, excitement, and mystery of the world we live in."

Rachel Carson, The Sense of Wonder

A Few Words About the Growing Problem of Children's Disconnection From Nature

"Without continuous hands-on experience, it is impossible for children to acquire a deep intuitive understanding of the natural world that is the foundation of sustainable development. A critical aspect of the present-day crisis in education is that children are becoming separated from daily experience of the natural world."

Robin C. Moore and Herb H. Wong,

Natural Learning: Creating Environments for Rediscovering Nature's Way of Teaching

Educators and mental health professionals world-wide are becoming concerned that many of today's children are no longer able to spend unhurried hours exploring the natural world in the same ways that previous generations enjoyed. Research is showing that children need connections with the natural world as a regular part of their healthy growth and development (Crain, 2001; Kahn & Kellert, 2002; Moore & Wong, 1997; Nabhan & Trimble, 1999). Disconnection from nature is leading to increases in problems such as childhood obesity, children's dislike and even fear of the outdoors, and increased reliance on behavior-regulating medications (Louv, 2005; Rivkin, 1995; White, 2004).

Research shows a dramatic decline in the amount of time today's children spend outdoors. Hoffert and Sandberg (2000) site the following statistics: Between 1981 and 1997, the amount of time U.S. children aged six to eight spent playing outdoors decreased by four hours per week while the amount of time they spent indoors in school increased by almost five hours per week.

One result of the reduction of children's direct experiences with the natural world is the rise of what researchers refer to as biophobia, a fear of the natural world and environmental issues (Sobel, 1996). Research by Wilson (1994) and Simmons (1994), based on personal interviews with groups of children varying in age from preschool to age nine, found that the attitudes children expressed toward various aspects of the natural environment (rain, wildflowers, trees, birds) included more fear and dislike than appreciation, caring or enjoyment. Cohen and Horm-Wingerd (1993) believe that children's

unfounded fears and misconceptions about the natural environment develop when they have very little actual contact with living things and obtain most of their attitudes through the electronic media.

Many children no longer spend long, unstructured hours playing outdoors creating positive bonds with nature. Families and educators must now provide intentional experiences and create spaces that give children the opportunity to better understand and appreciate the natural world. Dimensions' teacher-researchers have documented much evidence of valuable skill development occurring across all learning domains as children spend daily time in well-designed outdoor spaces with nurturing adults (Miller, 2007). This is especially true for children with sensory integration challenges (Taylor, Kuo & Sullivan, 2001).

Excerpts from focus group interviews conducted with educators in Dimensions' research classrooms will be highlighted throughout this book. They provide glimpses into the profound changes that can occur when outdoor spaces become nurturing places for learning with nature. We hope this book will inspire you to bring these kinds of life-changing experiences to children as together you reconnect with the joys of the natural world.

Field-Tested Guiding Principles

The most wonderfully designed natural outdoor classroom will only be as effective for children as the adults who explore it with them. As developmental psychologist Lev Vygotsky taught years ago, children's learning takes place best as part of caring relationships with adults and with other children (Vygotsky, 1962). Adults who themselves delight in experiencing the natural world and understand the rich learning that can take place in natural outdoor spaces will greatly aid children's healthy growth and development. Dimensions' field-testing and research, as well as other research noted on page 50, shows great benefits across the curriculum for children who explore well-designed outdoor spaces with nurturing adults. Educators and families who encourage children to master new challenges, develop increasingly complex skills, and closely observe and appreciate the natural world will give children gifts that will last for a lifetime.

A new way of thinking may be needed for many educators and families as children begin to spend more and more time learning with nature. Outdoor time will come to be seen as more than "recess," and will instead be viewed as an invaluable part of each day's learning activities. Families will help children dress appropriately for outdoor time in all kinds of weather, and educators and administrators will build time in the outdoor classroom into daily schedules.

Adults who understand and support the rich learning that can take place in natural outdoor spaces will significantly aid children's healthy growth and development.

The Ten Principles

The ten guiding principles on the following page are based on years of Dimensions' field-testing, and represent a well-rounded mix of experiences that can and should occur outdoors for preschool and elementary children. Explanations and examples for each principle can be found on pages 6-35.

Adults who observe closely will celebrate the intellectual, physical, social and emotional growth that can take place for every child every day in the natural outdoor classroom. And, they will delight in sharing the wonder and awe that nature can inspire in each of us, no matter our age or where we live.

The Ten Guiding Principles

1. Divide the space into clearly delineated areas for different kinds of activities.

2. Include a complete mix of activity areas.

   Recommended Areas: (Try to include all of these areas.)

   A. An entry feature

   B. An open area for large-motor activities

   C. A climbing/crawling area

   D. A "messy materials" area

   E. A building area

   F. A nature art area

   G. A music and movement area

   H. A garden and/or a pathway through plantings

   I. A gathering area (A separate area, or one of the other larger areas could be used as a gathering area.)

   J. A storage area (This could be a separate area, or storage could be included within each area as needed.)

   Supplemental Areas: (Try to include at least one of these areas.)

   K. A water area

   L. A dirt-digging area

   M. A sand area

   N. A wheeled-toy area

   O. An area for swings or other dynamic equipment

   P. A greenhouse

3. Give areas simple names.

4. Identify each area with a sign or other visual clues.

5. Be sure every area is visible at all times.

6. Use a variety of natural materials, including trees and other live plants.

7. Choose elements for durability and low maintenance.

8. Maximize beauty and visual clarity in the over-all design.

9. Personalize the design with regional materials, and ideas from children and staff.

10. Be sure the space meets all regulatory standards for your region.

See page 49 for information on becoming a certified Nature Explore Classroom.

Examples and Explanations of Each Guiding Principle

1. Divide the space into clearly delineated areas for different kinds of activities.

What this means:

Designate a separate area in the outdoor space for each type of specific activity.

- Think of each area as a separate "room."

- Provide elements that serve as dividers between the areas.

- Make sure that one activity does not interfere with another. (For example, separate the area for running from the area where children are building with wooden blocks.)

- Separate quiet areas from louder ones.

Why this is important:

Children need order, especially children who are strong visual-spatial thinkers and children who have sensory integration challenges. Entering a space with ten distinct activity areas is easier to understand and more calming than entering a space with a jumble of many individual activities arranged indiscriminately. By providing clearly defined activity areas, children are empowered to make choices and plans on their own. These separate activity areas decrease conflicts among children and increase children's ability to focus on learning activities.

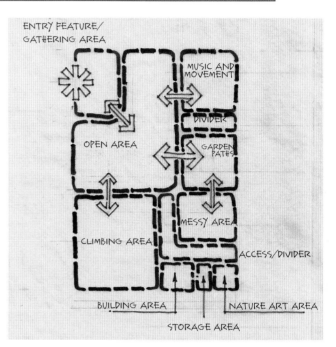

This diagram shows one example of an outdoor space that has been divided into areas.

Dividing the space into clearly defined activity areas increases children's ability to focus.

Ways to do this:

Divide areas by using materials that will inspire learning. Here are some **IDEAS** from which to choose. You might use one or many of these.

IDEA: Change the surface between areas to help children understand where one area begins and another ends. For example, change from grass to wood chips.

IDEA: Use low plant materials between areas. Aromatic plants like anise (in warm parts of the country), or spice bush (in colder climates) can divide areas while giving children interesting scents, colors, shapes and textures to explore. Be sure to choose plants that are non-toxic.

IDEA: Construct low walls out of brick. Enlist the help of a local sculptor or brick mason.

IDEA: Construct a low earth berm between two areas.

IDEA: Install low fences made from natural materials like willow (above) or sticks or pickets.

2. Include a complete mix of activity areas.

Recommended Areas: (Try to include all of these areas.)

A. An entry feature

What this means:

Provide a visual clue that lets children know they are entering a special place.

Why this is important:

A special entry feature helps children stop and focus attention on the outdoor space. Entry features with some depth to them (an arbor to walk through, for example) encourage thoughtful entry into the space instead of a "mad dash" to get to new activities.

Ways to do this:

There are many ways to call attention to the entrance to your outdoor space, some simple and some more complex. Here are a few **IDEAS** from which to choose:

IDEA: Create an arbor to walk through.

IDEA: Create a simple overhead feature with poles and fabric. This often works well in home childcare settings, or small spaces.

IDEA: Use a surface texture at the entry area that is different from surfaces in other areas. For example, use stone, tree "cookies", or concrete stamped with leaf prints as in the photo above.

A. (continued)

IDEA: **Attach interesting elements** onto entry gates. These can be changed from time-to-time using ideas from children.

IDEA: **Place containers of flowers** or ornamental grasses next to entry gates or grow vines or flowering plants directly on fences.

B. An open area for large-motor activities

What this means:

Keep one area of your outdoor space open so that children have plenty of room for large movement. This area is often called the "action area."

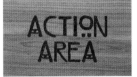

Why this is important:

Children need enough space to run, jump, dance, or play active games. Designating one space just for active play is important for children's health and well-being, especially in light of dramatically increased rates of childhood obesity and diabetes.

Ways to do this:

This space should be designed so that the active play does not "spill over" into quieter areas, such as the building area, and cause conflicts between children. It is ideal if this area can be covered with grass that can withstand much traffic. As part of regular maintenance, this grass will have to be reseeded or sodded periodically. The idea is not to have "perfect" grass but to provide enough coverage so that the ground is not overly muddy.

IDEA: **A large, grassy open area** will provide children with a place to run, jump or dance. It can also serve double-duty as a gathering area.

C. A climbing/crawling area

What this means:

Provide an area where children can crawl through and/or climb up designated elements. This area might be called the "climbing area" or the "climbing and crawling area."

Why this is important:

As children grow and develop they need to successfully master physical challenges in order to gain self-confidence and a sense of control over their environments. Learning how to maneuver their bodies in a variety of settings helps children gain skills that keep them safer. Looking at the world from multiple perspectives (gazing down from up high, or peering through a crawl-through log, for example) strengthens children's thinking in ways that support mathematical and visual-spatial skills.

Ways to do this:

Many programs have already invested in commercial equipment that is designed for climbing or crawling like the structure below.

If these structures meet safety standards and are installed correctly with appropriate fall-zone material underneath, they can provide children with appropriate challenges and experiences. Alternatives or supplements to this type of equipment are illustrated in the **IDEA** photos below and on the next page.

IDEA: Platforms installed around or near a tree give children a safe venue for climbing and interacting with nature at the same time. In the photo above left, sturdy tree-branch poles are placed vertically and horizontally, and children drape sheer weather-proof fabric to create changeable "rooms."

C. (continued)

IDEA: Tree stumps installed carefully provide a safe challenge for children to master as they practice jumping. Be sure to provide surfacing that meets safety regulations.

IDEA: Crawl-through logs help children explore the concept of inside and outside, and give them a glimpse into the inner-workings of a tree trunk. A translucent crawl-through tunnel that goes through a hill can reveal the "underground" to children. (See page 33.)

IDEA: Balance beams made from natural materials provide a nice alternative to hard plastic or steel products.

D. A "messy materials" area

What this means:

Create an area covered with wood chips or mulch where children can dig, carry heavy objects such as sections of tree stumps, and explore other "messy" materials from time-to-time like bales of hay or pumpkins.

Why this is important:

Today's children have fewer and fewer opportunities to interact with wild, natural areas that allow for free exploration and experimentation. Children's ability to "be messy" is also being restricted more and more as much of their time is spent either indoors or in manicured outdoor settings. A well-designed "messy materials" area can encourage children to use their imaginations, experiment with a variety of natural objects, practice carrying heavy objects, and feel a sense of accomplishment and personal mastery over the environment. Children with sensory integration challenges often excel in this area and gain skills in self-control and relaxation after being given enough opportunities to use large muscles to dig or carry heavy objects from place-to-place. The good news for adults is that the design of this area keeps "messiness" manageable since children actually stay relatively clean even as they immerse themselves in the wood chips or mulch.

"Messy materials" areas can help children gain a sense of accomplishment and personal mastery over the environment.

Ways to do this:

Fill an area with mulch or wood chips that are meant for use with children. Allow enough space for children to work in groups, maneuver large materials and use creativity. Surround the area with a barrier that is able to contain the mulch. **IDEAS** for barriers include logs or low brick walls like the ones on these pages.

Provide natural, heavy materials that children can carry and stack, such as sections of tree stumps, or tree cookies.

IDEA: Use low brick walls, logs or large stones to provide barriers for mulch.

D. (continued)

From time-to-time add new but temporary materials to this area using **IDEAS** like the ones below.

IDEA: Bring in longer log pieces occasionally to provide children with a new challenge.

IDEA: Provide seasonal items like pumpkins for children to explore.

IDEA: Let children create with long willow poles. Poles should be used with adult supervision, and only when children are developmentally ready to understand how to move them safely.

IDEA: Add hay bales, small rakes and child-sized wheelbarrows.

IDEA: Provide small hand tools so that children can dig in the mulch.

"You know, Logan and I have a little standing joke. I start a sentence for him by saying, 'If you ever feel worried, or bored, or you're upset, or things just don't feel right, you can always go outside'…And he finishes the sentence for me by saying, 'and get dirty!' Logan was not a 'get dirty' kind of kid. He was pretty tidy. But he connected with something new outdoors. He had a real love for learning about animals. He became an eagle expert. He brought in a book that he'd written about eagles. He made eagles' nests everywhere in the messy materials area and inside. This carried throughout the year. He moved like an eagle. And he was so very good at it. He came back this year as a first grader to visit the kindergarten class and he wanted to do the eagle dance and I think that was so valuable for the other children to see."

Teacher Suzan Haley, from a focus group interview

E. A building area

What this means:

Provide a hard-surfaced area where children can build with natural wooden blocks.

Why this is important:

Indoor spaces often cannot provide enough room for children to experiment with block construction, and outdoor spaces allow for a different kind of experience. Noise is not as much a factor outdoors as indoors, since the noise from falling block structures is absorbed outside in a way that is not possible indoors. Often children who are reluctant to build indoors are more willing to try this activity outside. Building with blocks provides many chances to strengthen visual-spatial, mathematical and abstract thinking. Providing blocks outdoors that are different from the typical blocks found inside classrooms gives children a chance to experiment in new ways. Additionally, including a building area in the outdoor classroom can often provide a chance for children in elementary grades to continue this important activity even after their indoor classrooms no longer provide such experiences.

A flat surface covered with a hard material like this "tree cookie" flooring provides an ideal setting for children to build with blocks outdoors and gain an appreciation for patterns in nature.

Ways to do this:

Make sure the area designated for building is a flat surface. Cover the surface with a hard material like stone or "tree cookies" set in a special grout. Using materials like large tree cookies for this flooring surface helps to delineate individual sections for children to build in, thus cutting down on conflicts between children. Adding laminated photos of block constructions, or even laminated photos of great works of architecture, will give children ideas to inspire more productive and creative work. You may want to design two separate building areas next to each other, each containing a different type of block.

IDEA: Create two small building areas next to each other. In the photos on the left, one area contains rectangular blocks made from four different types of woods, and the other contains organic "tree blocks" made from pieces of tree branches.

F. A nature art area

What this means:

Provide an area where children can use materials from nature to create patterns and works of art. This is also a place where materials that encourage children to sketch, such as clipboards and paper, might be stored.

Why this is important:

As children work with natural materials such as sticks, pine cones or leaves, and arrange them into patterns or mosaic-like pictures, they develop close observation skills, classification skills, and a sense of appreciation for the beauty of the natural world. As children handle these natural materials they also gain understanding of weight, mass, texture and shape. In addition, if children are encouraged to sketch natural features in the outdoor classroom, they notice details that they might otherwise miss. Children who physically explore the space by walking through pathways or moving from area to area, then draw a map of their path, are often able to successfully put paper to pencil in a way that they are otherwise unable to do. For many predominantly visual-spatial thinkers, this type of activity can serve as a wonderful link to written literacy activities (Miller, 2007).

Ways to do this:

Provide storage for art materials such as paper, pencil, clipboards, clay, chalk or watercolor paints. Encourage children to use natural materials such as pine cones, feathers, rocks or small sticks to create patterns or mosaics. Provide a table or hard surface where children can work.

IDEA: Providing clipboards and paper and pencils encourages children to develop close observation skills, strengthen eye-hand coordination and develop an appreciation for the beauty of nature.

G. A music and movement area

What this means:

Provide an area where children can experiment with making music and creating expressive movement.

Why this is important:

Music and movement experiences are vital to children's healthy development. Outdoor settings provide an ideal place for children to experiment with musical and movement expression. Outdoor music and movement areas provide a place in children's lives where they are able to make music and dance in an unstructured way, allowing for improvisation and creativity.

Concerns about noise are not as great outdoors as they are indoors, and room for storage of musical instruments is often larger in outdoor spaces. Well-equipped music and movement areas allow children to learn about sound, pitch, rhythm and tonality on their own; learn how to manipulate a variety of musical instruments; and experience concepts related to physics. Using musical instruments made from natural plant materials gives children a chance to experience the richness of nature and to learn about people and cultures world-wide that use these types of instruments.

A designated open space or performance stage specifically designed for free movement encourages children to move in ways of their own choosing in response to the environment surrounding them. Nature inspires creative movement with the rich patterns found in trees and plants, animals and insects, wind, water and weather.

Pairing the music and movement areas is natural. Children can express musical concepts by moving their bodies to music. In turn, children can express movement concepts by playing musical instruments.

IDEA: Marimbas provide children an opportunity to experiment with pitch and rhythm. Large marimbas should be permanently installed to guard against theft, and made from sturdy all-weather materials like ipé wood. Marimbas can be found in a variety of sizes.

G. (continued)

Ways to do this:

If space is limited, music and movement areas may be designed on the periphery of the open area so that as musical instruments are played, other children may dance or move creatively in the open area. If more space is available, a separate "performance stage" may be created in the movement and music area. Larger musical instruments such as marimbas should be permanently installed, but smaller ones like rain sticks could be stored in locking storage cabinets. Laminated photographs of people from around the world playing natural instruments could be posted on the front of the storage cabinet.

Provide a variety of non-electronic musical instruments made from plant materials. Use only instruments that are played by shaking, striking or plucking, not by blowing, since this will guard against passing germs from one child to another.

In addition to musical instruments, provide loose materials, like colorful scarves, that will inspire children to dance or move in interesting ways. These materials can be kept with the instruments in the locking storage cabinet.

IDEA: Scarves provide inspiration to encourage children to move in interesting ways, perhaps mimicking the motion of trees, grasses, birds or wind.

IDEA: Use log drums, shakers, rain sticks or chimes.

H. A garden and/or a pathway through plantings

What this means:

Provide a garden area where children can experience planting and harvesting flowers or vegetables, and/or a pathway for children to walk that takes them through a variety of low grasses, flowers or bushes.

Why this is important:

Interacting with natural vegetation helps children connect with the wonders of nature, learn about natural systems and seasons, and develop keen observation skills. When children are able to help plant, care for and harvest a garden, they learn a sense of responsibility and often develop increased appreciation for eating fresh produce if vegetables or fruits are grown (Pothukuchi, 2004). In programs where space is limited, or where it is not possible to take on the task of growing a garden, creating pathways through natural vegetation is an alternative that still provides children with a chance to interact with grasses or flowers. Walking through pathways bounded by beautiful natural vegetation on either side can give children a sense of being alone even though they still are in sight of supervising adults. Asking children to sketch their route through the pathway increases their visual-spatial skills and is an interesting task children often enjoy. Designing the pathway so that it contains shallow slopes to walk up and down will provide children with a manageable physical challenge to master. In programs with enough space, it would be ideal if both a garden and a pathway could be created since each experience provides something unique and valuable for children's development. Gardening is especially helpful for all learning styles, since it provides stimulation for all senses.

"We had an experience on the outdoor classroom with a very large spider who had made a web, and the children discovered it and came and got the teachers and said, 'Oh come look.' And here are children running to see the spider, and then another child knew that there was a poster of spiders inside and ran in and got it and brought the poster outside so we could identify what kind of spider it was. And I thought, you know what, five years ago we wouldn't have been doing that. Five years ago they would have been asking us to stomp on it and get rid of it."

Teacher Tina Reeble , from a focus group interview

Ways to do this:

A garden area can be designed very simply by marking out an area of ground that is reserved for planting. Involve children in the design of the garden area as much as possible. Children can help choose the kinds of seeds that will be planted, and create signs that mark each type of growing plant. It usually works best if this area is on the perimeter of the outdoor space so that children are not tempted to run through the garden to get to another area.

To save space and to provide a way for children to see growing plants at eye level, gardens can be designed to include terraces. Be sure to locate the garden as close to a water source as possible. Locate taller-growing plants near the garden's edge so as not to hide children from view.

Pathways can also be created near the edges of the outdoor classroom, or between other areas. If one area of the outdoor classroom already has a natural slope to it, this might be the ideal place to create a pathway. If no natural slope is present, creating low earth berms will provide children with challenging but manageable terrain to negotiate. Children's ideas can be enlisted in the design of the pathway. Encourage children to move stones in a variety of ways to try out possible pathway routes before choosing a permanent solution. Older children might create drawings of possible pathway routes. To create a "secret garden" feel, construct paths 12-18 inches wide through plants that are 3-3 ½ feet tall. Using natural grasses works well.

IDEA: Surround the garden area with a fence to protect it from children running in nearby areas.

IDEA: Involve children in designing pathways through natural plantings.

"The garden helped us learn about collecting seeds and recognize that something that might look dead could become a whole new garden. Children gathered seeds off the dead plants, and even now when they look at the sunflowers, they know to say, 'Boy, those are seeds.' And they learn that they can plant their own food right here. It's so valuable. A lot of people talked about how children were eating foods that they've never eaten before. The toddlers were thinking green peppers were just so delicious... and they were. I must say there's a very big difference in having grown your own food as compared to buying it in a store."

Teacher Holly Murdoch, from a focus group interview

I. A gathering area

What this means:

Provide an area that is large enough for an entire class to gather at one time.

Why this is important:

A gathering area provides a place where teachers can meet with groups for a variety of reasons. At the beginning of their time in the outdoor classroom, teachers can help children make individual choices about which areas to explore that day. Groups can also meet together at the end of their outdoor time to share individual discoveries and learning that occurred. Special events, such as group sing-alongs or visits from resource people, can take place in a gathering area.

Ways to do this:

In large spaces a separate gathering area can be designed near the entry. Materials such as wooden decking, a grouping of benches, or concrete imprinted with leaf shapes might be used. In smaller outdoor classrooms, one of the other areas (usually the open area) may be used as a place to gather.

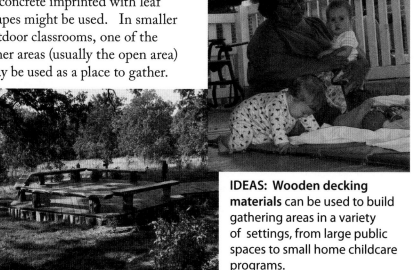

IDEAS: Wooden decking materials can be used to build gathering areas in a variety of settings, from large public spaces to small home childcare programs.

J. A storage area

What this means:

Provide an area for storage of loose materials, and/or provide separate storage units within certain areas.

Why this is important:

Children need easy access to loose materials like blocks, shovels or scarves, and adults need a way to store materials that doesn't involve trips back and forth from the indoors each day. Making materials readily accessible to children at their level will help ensure a more complete learning experience in the outdoor classroom.

Ways to do this:

If the space is large enough, a separate storage area can be designated for storage of items that can rotate throughout the space. Purchasing a commercial storage shed or similar unit for this purpose works well. In smaller spaces this larger unit may not be desirable. In either case, it is important to provide low, all-weather shelving for storage in areas such as the building area, the messy materials area and the music area. It would be ideal if these storage shelves were made from wood that could withstand the outdoors. If theft is a concern, storage shelves should have doors that fold back and latch open during day use, then unfold and lock at night.

Another aspect of storage that must not be overlooked is a place indoors to store clothing. Children need space to hang outerwear. Adults need places to store extra items for children who may have forgotten coats, mittens or boots, or need to change soiled clothing.

Supplemental Areas: (Try to include at least one of these areas.)

The following areas, while all valuable, may be more difficult to implement than the recommended areas. Individual differences in space, climate and staff wishes will determine which of these areas will work well in your outdoor classroom.

K. A water area

What this means:

Provide an area where children can safely experiment with water and its properties.

Why this is important:

Hands-on activities allow children to experience and change the flow of water, observe water currents, discover that some objects sink and others float, or predict whether a leaf will be propelled down a waterway faster than a feather. These early science experiences help children develop and internalize an understanding of the physical laws of nature. Watching how materials like sand or dirt change with the addition of water helps children learn about transformation of objects and the difference between solids and liquids.

Ways to do this:

There are many ways to include water in your outdoor space, some more elaborate than others. Be sure that whatever you choose does not involve water that stands for more than a few hours, or is deeper than regulatory codes for your region allow. Here are some ideas:

- Develop a separate water area by providing a purchased water feature that recirculates water and allows children to experiment with water flow. Add large moveable stones so that children can manipulate the direction and intensity of the water currents.

- As a lower-cost alternative, purchase a hand-pumped water feature or use a small water table that can be filled and drained each day.

- Instead of developing a separate water area, add water occasionally to a sand area or digging area by bringing in buckets of water or letting a hose trickle for a few minutes.

- Bring small buckets of water and paint brushes outside and encourage children to "paint" with water on concrete or other hard surfaces. On warm days, notice the process of evaporation.

IDEA: As an alternative to a separate water area, add water to the sand area sometimes.

IDEA: A recirculating shallow water feature encourages children to experiment.

L. A dirt-digging area

What this means:

Provide an area where children can dig directly into soil.

Why this is important:

Fewer and fewer children have the opportunity to spend time simply digging in dirt anymore. Experiencing the rich feeling and aroma of soil can be calming and beneficial to children, as well as adults. Working with dirt (soil) gives children a chance to experience a texture that is different from sand. In digging areas children may also have the chance to discover insects or earthworms in the soil.

> "There's something about the digging area that's like a blank piece of paper or chalkboard. I've seen kids take sticks and make letters. It's just such a contrast, the natural materials that they can spell things with against the dark background. It's almost like a writing board."
>
> *Teacher Kristin Holmes, from a focus group interview*

Ways to do this:

Create a small square or rectangular area bounded by a brick or wooden perimeter. Construct seats made from bricks or stone around the edge of the rectangle so that children may sit and dig without becoming completely covered with dirt or mud.

IDEA: Plant brightly colored flowers outside the border of the digging area. Use wood, stone or brick to create borders. Add small square seats in a few places along the perimeter.

M. A sand area

What this means:

Provide an area for experimentation with sand.

Why this is important:

Working with sand provides a different tactile experience than working with dirt (soil). Sand areas provide ideal settings for positive social interaction.

Ways to do this:

If there is enough space, creating a sand box large enough for a number of children to explore at one time is ideal. Sand boxes can be purchased commercially, or can be created by pouring a concrete perimeter. If space allows, creating an "L" shaped sandbox allows more children to work at one time with fewer conflicts. Create a sand box that can be covered at night to keep out animals. Canvas pieces work well for covers and can be rolled up during the day.

IDEA: As an alternative to plastic toys, add natural materials like tree stumps to the sand area. Try giving children galvanized metal buckets instead of plastic ones.

IDEA: Create sand areas that are large enough to encourage group interaction. Here children are working cooperatively to create the "Grand Canyon."

N. A wheeled-toy area

What this means:

Provide a separate space for children to ride small wheeled toys. This space is usually created only for children kindergarten-aged and younger.

Why this is important:

Providing an area where children can manipulate wheeled toys away from the flow of the rest of the outdoor classroom gives them another chance to use large muscles. If a slight slope is designed into the wheeled-toy pathway, this provides another challenge for children to master.

Ways to do this:

Be sure that the wheeled-toy area does not interfere with other areas. Some outdoor classrooms are designed so that a wheeled-toy track rings the perimeter of the space, and this often leads to conflicts as children walking from one area to another collide with riding children. Creating a meandering or slightly sloping pathway for wheeled toys provides children with just enough physical challenge to keep them engaged. Wheeled-toy paths need to be hard-surfaced with smooth materials such as concrete or flagstone. This area is more challenging to implement because of the need for space, and because only a limited age-range can use the area at one time. Some programs located in colder climates have indoor gymnasiums where children can ride wheeled toys and may not choose to provide an outdoor area for this purpose. Other programs, even with limited space, may choose to provide a small wheeled-toy pathway where only a few children will ride at one time.

O. An area for swings or other dynamic equipment

What this means:

Provide a separate area where children can use swings or other equipment that moves, such as spring rockers. Be sure that this area meets all regulatory guidelines for your region.

Why this is important:

Dynamic movable equipment provides children with valuable ways to experience the sensation of moving through space. Swings can provide individual experiences, or valuable opportunities for children to work together and strengthen social skills.

Ways to do this:

First, be sure that any equipment chosen meets all safety guidelines for your region. Proper installation of equipment is also vital.

There are generally two types of swings chosen: Single-axis swings designed to move back and forth; or multiple-axis swings designed to swing in any direction (like a tire swing). Swings take up a great deal of space on outdoor classrooms and require intense supervision, so are often not an ideal choice in many locations. If swings are desired, but space is limited, a tire swing might be the best option.

Spring rockers also provide children with the sensation of movement, and are often vehicles for imaginative play. Again, be sure equipment meets safety standards and is properly installed.

IDEA: Tire swings are a good choice if space is limited.

P. A greenhouse

What this means:

Provide a greenhouse that can be operated year-round.

Why this is important:

Greenhouses, whether large or small, give children a chance to closely observe, care for and enjoy flowers, vegetables or worm bins. Especially in colder climates, greenhouses provide children with a longer time period in which to interact with living plants.

Ways to do this:

There are many options and price-ranges for greenhouses. Most are made of either poly carbonate or glass. Either type works, but glass is generally more expensive. Some greenhouses can attach directly to your building, and others are designed to stand alone. If you have a stand-alone greenhouse it would be nice to have electricity and water available, but it is not always necessary.

One nice addition to a greenhouse (or a low-cost alternative to a greenhouse) is a worm bin. Worm bins help children practice caretaking as they learn to feed the worms, add peat and other materials to the bin and gently hold and watch the worms. Many children who have problems with anger and impulse control have been able to redefine themselves as nurturing individuals by being asked to care for a worm bin. See the following page for ideas on how to construct your own worm bin.

"The greenhouse provides a place for us to focus our experience on worms or dirt or seeds or bulbs, or how water gets from the bottom of the plant to the top of the plant. We've got the things right there. We've got the real life thing that we're touching, smelling, feeling, sometimes tasting, and then we can explore that further. We're either pulling it apart to see the pieces, we're sketching it, or we're adding it to the worm tank to find out what will happen next. 'Oh, they're going to decompose but the worms will eat it.' It's that learning environment that I appreciate so much."

Teacher Tina Reeble, from a focus group interview

Create a worm bin

Charuth Loth from Shadowbrook Farm (an organic community farm near Lincoln, Nebraska) has worked with many Dimensions Foundation research classrooms to create worm bins. She suggests the following steps:

1. Use a shallow bin made of metal, plastic or wood (with a waterproof bottom). A horse tank 4' x 6' works well.

2. If outside, worm bins need to be in temperatures ranging from 55 to 80 degrees F. Bins should be in shaded areas, and kept from freezing.

3. To keep bins from smelling, keep a 30:1 ratio (by volume) of carbon to nitrogen materials when filling the bin to create soil.

Possible Materials

Carbon	Nitrogen
Peat	Wet kitchen scraps (no meat or bones)
Newspaper	Green grass or garden waste
Brown paper bags	Coffee grounds
Dry leaves	Alfalfa pellets
Straw	
For example, use 30 times more ripped newspaper, leaves and peat moss than coffee grounds.	

4. Add worms such as red wigglers. Add a layer of dry material to cover the worms.

5. Add enough water to moisten every time you add carbon materials. Be careful to observe worms using up the nitrogen materials before you add more.

6. To make it possible to remove worm castings (droppings and dead worms), begin feeding worms on one end of the bin. After a few weeks, carefully lift some soil from the other end onto a screen on a tarp or plastic tablecloth. Remove any worms in the soil and put them back in the bin. Put soil through the screen. Use worm castings left on the screen as compost in a garden. Put the soil back in the worm box. In early spring worms lay eggs that look like tiny orange balls. Avoid disturbing the worm bin until the eggs hatch.

3. Give areas simple names.

IDEA: Choose a simple name for each area. Enlist children's help in naming areas.

What this means:

Simple names like "action area" are more understandable and appealing to children than names like "gross motor area."

Why this is important:

Giving areas simple, understandable names helps children remember the layout of the space, and empowers them to make their own plans to engage in different kinds of activities.

Ways to do this:

Listen to the words children use to describe various areas. For example, the name "messy materials" area was chosen for the area containing wood chips, sections of tree stumps and other loose materials because these were the words children used most frequently to describe the area. The name "action area" also came from children. The children in your program may choose different names. It can be helpful to post photos of children at work next to the name of each area.

4. Identify each area with a sign or other visual clues.

What this means:

Post permanent signs to identify the name of each area. Drawings could be included directly on signs to give children visual clues about how each area might be used.

In addition to signs, post laminated photographs that give children ideas for using the materials in an area.

Why this is important:

Posting signage and visual clues in each area is one more way to provide focus and clarity for children. Signage containing simple written words can also provide a link to literacy. Children who are developmentally ready to write words often enjoy drawing maps of the outdoor space, and labeling each area by writing its name.

Visual images that give children ideas for appropriate ways to use materials can provide a positive alternative to the violent visual images children sometimes pick up from television, movies or video games.

Ways to do this:

Secure wooden signs on posts, structures or fences. Laminate photos of children at work in the area, and secure to storage containers or to the bottom of signs.

IDEA: Post laminated photos of children's work to inspire creativity and appropriate use of materials. These photos can be changed periodically, and children can be enlisted to help choose new ideas to post. Here photos of mosaics made with natural materials are posted in the nature art area.

IDEA: Secure a sign with the name of the area onto posts or directly to structures. Be sure not to attach signs to live trees since this will harm them.

IDEA: Secure objects directly onto storage containers to give children visual clues for easy clean-up. Here children sort blocks by type of wood as they put them away. A labeled block of each type is secured above each section.

5. Be sure every area is visible at all times.

What this means:

There should not be any spaces in the outdoor classroom where children are hidden from an adult's view.

Why this is important:

In order to safely supervise children, adults need to be able to stand in any place on the outdoor classroom and see children in an unobstructed way. In very large spaces, more than one adult will be needed to provide adequate supervision.

Ways to do this:

Place large pieces of equipment along the perimeter of the space to avoid obstructing views. Avoid enclosures where children cannot be seen from the outside. Provide sheer, weather-proof fabric that allows children to create see-through treehouse "rooms."

Many spaces, such as the pathway through plantings, can give children a feeling of being in a "hidden" place when in reality they can still be seen by adults. Tall native grasses are a good choice to plant near pathways.

Giving children the sense of being in a "secret garden," while still maintaining safety, is a wonderful way to meet the needs of both children and adults.

IDEA: Plant tall native grasses to give children the feeling of being in a "hidden" space.

6. Use a variety of natural materials, including trees and other live plants.

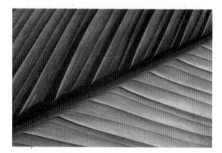  

What this means:

Try to use items made from natural materials like wood, stone or brick as much as possible, instead of relying solely on plastic or metal equipment. Find ways to incorporate live plant materials into the space whenever possible. Incorporate existing trees into the overall design.

Why this is important:

Children are becoming more and more disconnected from the textures, smells and beauty of the natural world. Using materials from nature as much as possible in the design of outdoor spaces can help reverse this trend. Incorporating plant materials, from grass to flowers to trees not only adds beauty and softness, but also provides many opportunities for children to learn about the colors, shapes, textures and patterns of nature; to observe seasonal changes; and to practice caretaking, nurturing behaviors. Live plant materials also attract interesting birds and insects for children to observe and enjoy.

6. (continued)

Ways to do this:

The "Explanations and Examples of Guiding Principles" section of this book gives multiple examples of ways to use natural materials as an alternate to metal or plastic structures. Also, as noted earlier, planting sturdy grass in an open area is an excellent start in bringing nature to children's daily lives.

Using plants as dividers between areas is another good strategy. Working with existing trees or planting new ones can lead to opportunities for level-change activities such as installing low platforms to surround a tree and simulate a "treehouse" experience. If new trees are planted, choosing both deciduous and evergreen will give children an opportunity to compare and contrast seasonal changes.

Choose plants for their interesting qualities, such as those that attract butterflies. Many plants have distinctive aromas or soft textures that children love, such as lamb's ear.

Creating a pathway surrounded on both sides by plant materials is another way of giving children daily contact with nature. If maintenance is an issue, planting sturdy grasses instead of harder-to-care-for flowers may be more feasible. If the space is already hard-surfaced throughout, large planter boxes may be used to add touches of nature in different areas.

7. Choose elements for durability and low maintenance.

What this means:

Whenever possible, choose equipment or plant materials that will require the least amount of maintenance and upkeep.

Why this is important:

The most beautiful outdoor space will quickly become an eye-sore if routine maintenance is not carried out on a regular basis. Most programs have limited resources and time for maintenance, so minimizing this task as much as possible is vital.

Ways to do this:

Think carefully about the resources for maintenance available at your site. Do you have access to water, and how often is it feasible to water plant material? If no water or limited water is available, plant native grasses, hardy shrubs or trees that require little watering. Think carefully about whether your program can support a full-fledged garden or whether a small "pizza garden" in a planter box filled with items that go into pizza, like oregano, basil, and cherry tomatoes, might best fill the bill. Less elaborate, but well-maintained areas will stand the test of time better than overly ambitious constructions that soon become worn-down. On the other hand, forming partnerships with volunteers outside your organization might make it possible to try more elaborate plans. See pages 38-39 for ideas on utilizing community volunteers to help with maintenance.

It should be noted that natural materials will need to be replaced or replanted at regular intervals. Try to include maintenance and replacement costs in your annual budget. Many materials, like "tree cookies" in the "messy materials" area, will naturally break or crumble over time. This is desirable, because it gives children a chance to watch natural processes at work. Items like these in the outdoor classroom should be replenished regularly, just like indoor equipment such as paper or pencils are regularly restocked.

IDEA: If you don't have the space or maintenance to support a full-fledged garden, try planting a small "pizza garden" like the one above. Here a little girl is smelling a basil plant.

IDEA: Plan to replace "loose parts" such as "tree cookies" periodically just as you restock disposable indoor materials.

8. Maximize beauty and visual clarity in the overall design.

What this means:

Be sure the over-all design of the space and the materials you choose are as aesthetically pleasing as possible. Keep "visual clutter" to a minimum. Carefully add only those visual clues, such as signage or laminated photos, that help children understand the layout of the space and how each area is meant to be used.

Why this is important:

Children respond positively to aesthetically pleasing spaces, and are more apt to engage in pro-social behaviors in beautiful settings. Research shows that incidents of vandalism decrease in public spaces that are aesthetically pleasing and well-maintained, compared to worn-down and unattractive spaces (Kelling & Coles, 1996).

Ways to do this:

By using a variety of natural materials with interesting textures and pleasing colors, the area will automatically be visually appealing. Since natural colors are more subtle than bright-colored play equipment, add a few touches of bold color with items like scarves for inspiring creative movement.

Trees and other plant materials can also add bright splashes of color to the space. Choosing color accents wisely and sparingly will guard against visual overload. Carefully choosing signage and a small number of laminated visual images for each area will also add to the clarity of the overall space.

IDEAS: Plant deciduous trees that will add bright splashes of seasonal color to the space (left). Add carefully chosen materials like bright fabric to accent the subtle colors of nature (above). Choose beautiful materials with interesting shapes and textures for children to explore in the nature art area (such as the rocks below).

9. Personalize the design with regional materials, and ideas from children and staff.

What this means:

As much as possible, use natural materials that are native to your area. Involve children, families, staff and others in the community in the design of the space.

Why this is important:

Each outdoor space should have a personality of its own. It should reflect the community of learners who will use it, and the interests and creative gifts of the larger community in which it is located. Using regional materials helps children develop a sense of place, and encourages increased observation skills.

Ways to do this:

Using the talents of local artists such as brick masons or painters can add to the beauty and interest of your outdoor space. (See pages 39-41 for ideas.) Incorporating materials from your own region into the design of your space will help children understand how the natural world and the built environment can work in harmony with each other.

IDEA: Pay close attention to children's interests when choosing materials. Chalk drawing is a favorite activity of the little girl in the photo above, so adults make sure plenty of chalk is available.

IDEA: Be sure to plant plenty of trees or flowers native to your region for children to explore.

9. (continued)

IDEA: Enlist the help of a local woodworker to create unique benches from regional wood. In these photographs from Nebraska, benches are being constructed from trees grown locally. The wood in the photo on the left comes from a bur oak tree that was hit by lightning.

IDEA: Help children interact in unique ways with natural regional plant materials. In these photographs from California, a bike path was constructed through grasses (left), and a translucent crawl-through tunnel was installed in a hillside filled with interesting vegetation (right).

9. (continued)

IDEA: Use the interests of teachers and staff to inspire children's learning. These photographs show sculptures and mosaics created out of natural materials by children and staff. The work was inspired by the teachers' interest in the work of artist and environmental sculptor, Andy Goldsworthy. Teachers shared some of Goldsworthy's books with children before beginning their collaborative creations.

IDEA: Find new uses for old materials. The photograph above is from a program with an outdoor space filled mostly with concrete. Grass was planted in a child's swimming pool as a way to bring more nature to children. Infants love to lie in it and feel the soft texture.

IDEA: Use materials that children find especially fascinating. In these photographs from Tennessee, children enjoy using bamboo pieces and materials collected in nearby woods to construct temporary sculptures (left).

10. Be sure the space meets all regulatory standards for your region.

What this means:

Work with the organization in your community responsible for regulating outdoor spaces to be sure that your plans meet all licensing standards. Be sure to have your plans reviewed before any construction begins. If licensing is not required for your organization, follow standards from national organizations such as The National Program for Playground Safety or the U.S. Consumer Product Safety Commission. Try to design the space so that it is as fully accessible as possible throughout.

Why this is important:

Safety, of course, is of paramount importance in an outdoor space. A certain amount of risk is inherent in outdoor play, and the goal is to minimize risk as much as possible without taking out all challenges for children. Adult supervision is a key factor in children's safe use of an outdoor space. As adults work with children to help them learn how to negotiate challenges and how to safely use materials and equipment, risks decrease. Children who have learned to safely master realistic physical challenges are less likely to suffer serious injury than children who have been overly protected from any physical risk.

Ways to do this:

If your program is one that must be licensed, contact your local licensing agency for guidance on meeting regional licensure standards. Publications like the Handbook for Public Playground Safety from the U.S. Consumer Product Safety Commission can also be helpful in answering questions about safety regulations. The Resources section on page 51 includes information on other national publications that give guidance on meeting safety standards and designing for accessibility.

Special Safety and Accessibility Considerations to Note:

All safety regulations are important, but the points below are worth special mention.

- Check fall zone heights and depth of cushioning surfaces under climbing, crawling and dynamic equipment.

- Make sure that no entrapment hazards exist in any of the structures or equipment on your outdoor space.

- Be sure that all equipment is installed according to manufacturer's specifications.

- Visit The National Center on Accessibility Web site for thoughts on how to make your space as accessible as possible. (See page 51 for more information.)

"I think it's important to have a large open area. I like to be able to move around out there and have all the open space. I think if we had the outdoor space so congested with all kinds of things it would become a real safety issue."

Teacher Julie Rose, from a focus group interview

Each outdoor setting is unique. Several factors that make your setting one-of-a-kind are outlined in this section. Thoughtful consideration of each of the following aspects can make the difference between an adequate space and a truly magical place for learning.

Age Considerations

Outdoor classrooms need to be designed with children's ages and developmental levels in mind. It is best that a separate space is designed for infants and toddlers, for example. If this is not possible, then time for infants and toddlers to be alone on the outdoor space should be scheduled carefully. If a space will be shared by many ages, materials will have to be chosen that do not cause undue safety concerns for younger children. Surrounding one or two of the areas that work well for the youngest children with a low fence or barrier could help infants and toddlers play safely in that space while older children explore other parts of the outdoor classroom that might be more challenging.

Think carefully about the ages and developmental levels of the children in your program, and be sure to provide enough appropriate challenges in your outdoor space to keep children engaged and motivated. Many materials, such as tree blocks and natural musical instruments, are open-ended enough that they can be used in increasingly complex ways by a wide range of ages. Continually adding and rotating "loose parts" to the outdoor space is another way to increase interest and age-appropriateness.

Meeting Individual Needs

Careful design can ensure that the space will work well for children with special needs and for all learning styles. Creating wheeled-toy paths that are at least 3 ½ feet wide, and building in transfer points on the platforms around trees, for example, will ensure that children in wheelchairs may interact successfully.

Designing louder, active spaces (like the action area or the music and movement area) and quieter, more individualized spaces (like the pathways through plantings or the nature art area) will give children a variety of choices to help meet their interests, needs and changing moods.

Planting trees that will grow into sheltering shapes, or creating living willow huts to provide children with a place to "get away from it all" is a wonderful strategy for meeting the needs of children who sometimes become over-stimulated by too much noise and commotion. If space allows, consider planting a small grove of trees such as redbuds or crapemyrtles.

IDEAS: Add loose parts such as milk crates to give children new challenges (left).

Plant a living willow hut to provide a place to "get away from it all" (right).

Climate Considerations

"Neither rain nor hail nor sleet nor snow nor heat of day nor dark of night…" might be a great credo for postal carriers, but it does not always transfer well to outdoor classrooms. There is no doubt that climatic conditions directly affect how outdoor space is used. The key is to think of ways to lessen the harsh effects of your climate and capitalize on the most pleasant ones.

If outdoor classrooms are able to be used on most days, in most kinds of weather, support from administrators, educators and parents is vital, as is proper clothing and physical design features such as:

Storage/transition areas for extra or special clothing. Designate a place where children can change into or out of snow-laden, rain-soaked or soiled clothing. Be sure to have extra clothing on hand that childen can borrow.

Shade trees and windbreaks. Planting large-growing shade trees will help cool children on hot days. Closely spaced evergreens can be planted along the edge of your outdoor classroom as a screen to block winter winds.

Overhead planes or roofs. If intense sun is a factor, be sure to find ways to provide protection for children if needed in addition to shade trees.

IDEA: Construct a simple pergola such as the one on the left to provide a source of shade.

All-weather surfaces. If heavy rainfall is typical in your region, be sure to choose surfaces that drain quickly and do not get slippery. If heat is an issue, choose light-colored surfaces. Dark-colored surfaces will provide more rapid snow and ice melt in areas where this is desired.

Changes in weather provide a great opportunity for children to become comfortable with natural cycles. Consider designing in or adding some of the following ways to take advantage of the climate in your area.

- Rain: Replace a building downspout with a decorative rain chain. Encourage childen to splash in puddles and delight in playing in the rain.

- Snow and ice: Help children create snow or ice sculptures and structures.

- Wind: Hang fabrics, pennants, kites, wind chimes, or whirligigs.

- Sun: Place sun-sensitive paper or dark construction paper on hard surfaces to make solar prints. Place natural objects on top and watch what happens as the sun bleaches the paper.

- Heat: Experiment with water and evaporation. Place clay in the sun and watch how it "bakes."

Seasonal changes can also be fascinating as flowers and leaves change color, and children discover the concept of deciduous versus evergreen. Solar angles are interesting to watch as shadow lengths change over the course of the year, and beautiful patterns of light occur.

Working With Community Resources

Taking time to think about who you will work with in designing, building and maintaining your space is a key part of creating a nurturing and inspiring place for children and adults to enjoy. Each community has its own personality. Finding the professionals, volunteers, artists and artisans who make your community special will help you honor the uniqueness of your region.

Working With a Design Professional

Since the circumstances of outdoor spaces vary considerably, not all programs will need to employ a design professional. It may be possible for you to handle simple additions or modifications to your outdoor classroom in-house. When things get more complicated, a professional designer's services can be quite helpful, especially if your outdoor space is new.

The product of collaboration with a professional can vary. A concept sketch showing sizes and locations of spaces and objects may be sufficient if you have a local builder, volunteers or staff capable of implementing the design. If this resource is not available, or if your administration requires that the implementation work be competitively bid, then a more detailed set of drawings will be needed. This aspect should be understood at the project's outset and will affect the selection of the consultant. You have several types of professionals from which to choose:

Architect: If you are designing or renovating a building, an architect will usually be engaged. Master planning may be a part of their task, and often exterior spaces such as outdoor classrooms are included in that effort. The design of learning facilities may be a particular practice type of a firm, but it should not be assumed that outdoor learning environments are an area of expertise. Ask about the particular experience of the firm members who will be doing the design work.

Landscape Architect: These professionals are best suited to designing exterior spaces. They are trained to deal with site aspects such as natural systems and drainage patterns. As with architects, not all landscape architects have experience in the design of exterior learning environments, so they should be interviewed to learn their particular strengths. Like architecture, landscape architecture practice is regulated by most states, and professional registration is often required.

Playground Designer: These professionals can be a good resource for ADA compliance, but since their knowledge is often strongest in the area of manufactured equipment, they may not be the best choice for overall planning. Sometimes a professional of this type who works independently and is not associated with a particular company may have an impressive portfolio and be worth considering. If your organization or local government authority requires professional design registration or licensure for obtaining building permits, check to make sure the individual meets that requirement prior to engaging them.

A highly desirable skill, regardless of the type of professional you choose, is the ability to define a positive process the design team will follow. Seek someone who is process-oriented, listens to your ideas and concerns carefully, and is not simply imposing their desires on your space. Since there is a particular set of program guidelines (the ten guiding principles in this book) and a varied set of stakeholders (administration, staff, children and parents) there is much for a designer to consider. A well-understood collaborative process provides a path to a design solution that all participants can embrace.

Working With Volunteers

Enlisting the help of volunteers needs to be handled with care. Being sure that volunteers have the skills needed for the task assigned is very important. Sometimes well-meaning volunteers offer to work in areas beyond their abilities, and this can lead to frustration for all, and possibly even safety concerns. A key part of developing a personalized design plan for an outdoor space is assessing the skills and talents of volunteers and agreeing on appropriate jobs. Sometimes paying for professional services for key jobs actually saves time and money in the long run.

IDEA: **If you have a Keep America Beautiful affiliate or an Alliance for Community Trees organization** in your community, they might provide volunteers to help plant or maintain trees or flowers in your space. Sororities or fraternities on college campuses are often looking for service projects, as are high school students in many areas who are required to complete a number of community service hours. Some of the parents, grandparents or staff members in your program may be master gardeners who would love to help create and maintain your garden or the plantings around the pathway.

IDEA: **Local nurseries, community extension agencies, community foresters, agricultural students or owners of organic farms** are often great resources for identifying which trees, flowers or grasses will grow well in your area and be desirable for use with children.

Working With Artists and Craftspeople in Your Community to Create a Unique Space

Finding talented people in your own community who can help you personalize the look and feel of your outdoor classroom is a wonderful strategy. It is often cost-saving as well. Here are a number of **IDEAS** for incorporating the knowledge and talents of local artists, or craftspeople, into your setting:

IDEA: Work with a local musician to help you create interesting temporary instruments.

39

IDEA: Create a mural. Find a local artist who will work with children (or with children's ideas) to create a mural on your outdoor space that tells the story of who you are as a community of learners. Some organizations may have staff members who are able to carry out this project. Some colleges or universities may be able to connect you to art students who could work on this project as part of an internship. In public settings, such as parks, murals could be created as community-wide projects.

IDEA: Create a low brick wall or sculpture. Work with a local sculptor or brick-layer to create a low brick wall as a divider for one of your areas, or create an interactive sculpture for children to explore in your art area.

Working With Artists and Craftspeople in Your Community (cont.)

IDEA: Invite musicians or dancers to perform in your outdoor space to inspire children to find new ways of expressing themselves through connections with nature. In the photos above and right, musicians are inspiring children to explore natural instruments. In the photos below, two professional dancers and a child are mimicking the shapes of trees with their bodies.

Creating Your Plan

The following questions will help you begin the design or redesign of your outdoor space. You will most likely not be able to address all of these items, and some may well be in conflict with each other. The idea is to help you be aware of these factors so you will be able to understand their impact and set priorities.

1. Who will be on your design team? Be sure to involve children's ideas and interests, along with those of staff, administrators, parents and interested community members. Think about resource people who might have valuable talents to contribute to the process, and remember to include ideas from people responsible for maintenance. Decide on how much you will need to involve a professional designer, and what type of designer you will use.

2. Decide on a reasonable budget. What is the minimum you have to spend? What services and materials will you try to have donated? Will you need to implement your plan in phases or can it be implemented all at once?

3. The following site-related questions will be especially helpful to address when designing new spaces, but many will also be relevant during the redesign process:

- Does the entry/exit need to be in proximity to a building? In schools, for example, it would be ideal for the indoor classroom to open directly onto the outdoor classroom.

- Is the space located in close proximity to other activities? For example, in a park setting, there could be potential hazards in locating the outdoor classroom too close to a baseball field. Avoid conflicts with day-to-day functions such as drop off/pick up locations.

- What are the general slopes of the space like? In choosing a new location, try to find higher ground and avoid areas that are always wet from drainage or areas where adding new materials will block drainage.

- Are there existing trees? Be sure to incorporate these into the design. How can you best take advantage of shade from mature trees? Will more trees need to be planted? If working with existing trees, make plans to protect trees during construction so soil does not become so compacted that roots are damaged. Avoiding soil compaction in the design of new spaces helps ensure survival of newly planted trees and other plant materials.

- How will there be access for maintenance equipment such as mowers?

- How can the site best take advantage of the climate, and factors such as sun/shade, rain/snow, heat/cold?

Paying close attention to children's ideas and interests will help you create a design that really works.

4. Will utilities such as water or electricity be available if needed?

5. Will restroom facilities be available in close proximity?

6. What areas will you include in your plan? Where will you locate the recommended areas listed in the guiding principles? Do you have enough room for each area? For example, the "messy materials" area might need more room than the nature art area. What will you use to divide and delineate the spaces? Will you add any of the supplemental areas from the guidelines? If so, which ones? Where will you locate these? How will you ensure that children will be visible at all times?

7. Who will implement your design? Will you need paid help or can all implementation be completed by volunteers?

8. What other issues need to be addressed so everyone will be comfortable with the final design plan?

9. How will you provide activities to help people look forward to using the new space? Consider providing staff workshops, family gatherings or community celebrations.

"We should keep asking everyone, 'Why not have a garden?' We can read children books, we can have our indoor science tables, which are both wonderful, but to actually be able to go outside in the real environment and experience the life process from planting a seed to going all the way through to the harvest is amazing. Children are able to use much more of their senses, to feel, to see, to hear. It makes it exactly what you would want for a learning experience, one that I think is much more meaningful."

Teacher Julie Rose, from a focus group interview

"It's perfect that we created the messy area under the big tree because it's partially shaded and partially sunny. It's also fun when the leaves fall and children can try to catch them."
Teacher Chris Kiewra, from a focus group interview

Be sure to design in plenty of opportunities for children to enjoy the simple yet profound pleasures of nature.

Ideas for Specific Situations

I n this section are ideas for a few of the many ways that the guiding principles might be implemented in creating new spaces or working with challenges in existing ones. Whether you are working with a very small private space and a tiny budget, or a large public space with plenty of funding, the guiding principles can help you create a nurturing place that will help children learn with nature as they play. With enough commitment and creativity, wonderful experiences for children can be provided in any outdoor setting.

Creating New Spaces

On this page, and the following two, are sample drawings that show ways the guiding principles might be used in the design of new spaces of varying sizes. It is important to state clearly that these are only ideas, and are not meant to be followed exactly. You will want your space to be uniquely yours, reflecting who you are as an organization or community, and what you most value and believe. Areas are labeled in black and equipment and features are labeled in dark red.

Sample Plan: 2,500 square feet

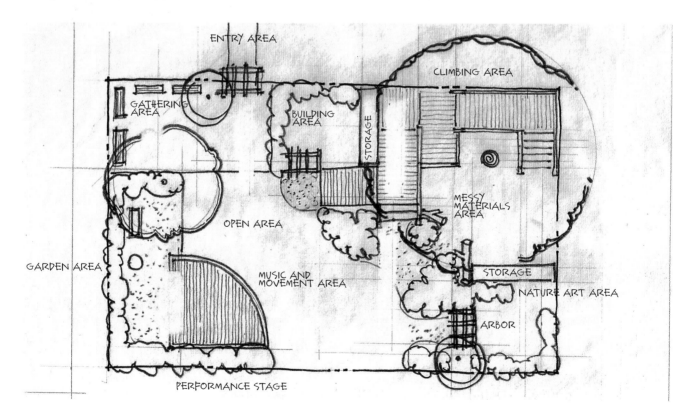

Sample Plan: 5,000 square feet

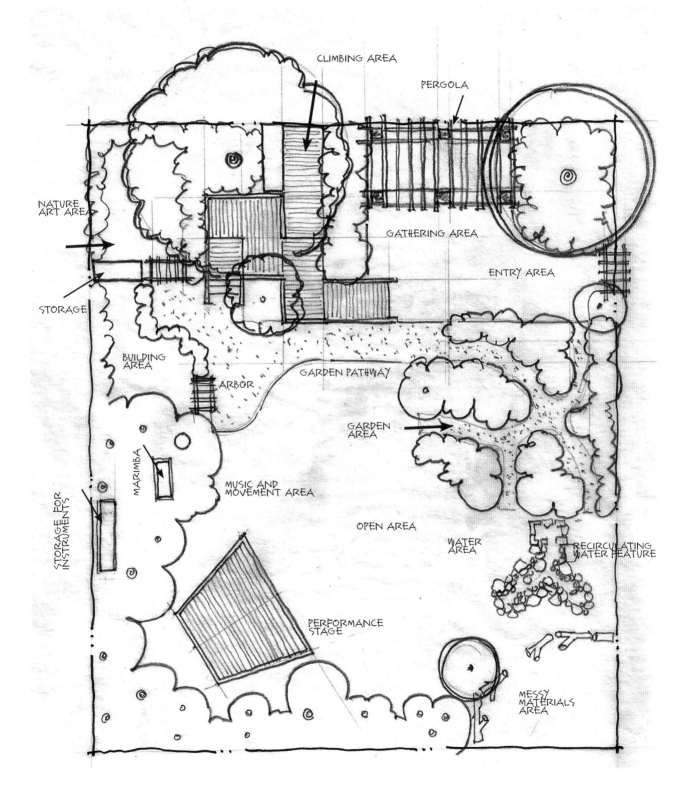

CLIMBING AREA

PERGOLA

NATURE
ART AREA

STORAGE

GATHERING AREA

ENTRY AREA

BUILDING
AREA

GARDEN PATHWAY

ARBOR

GARDEN
AREA

MARIMBA

MUSIC AND
MOVEMENT AREA

STORAGE FOR
INSTRUMENTS

OPEN AREA

WATER
AREA

RECIRCULATING
WATER FEATURE

PERFORMANCE
STAGE

MESSY
MATERIALS
AREA

Sample Plan: 10,000 square feet

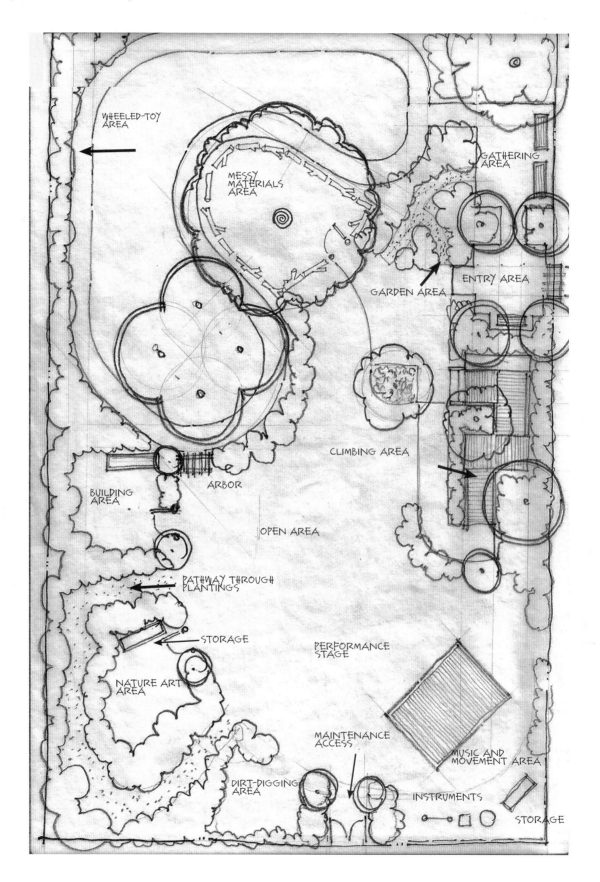

Working With Challenges in Existing Spaces

Lack of Natural Vegetation

Some existing outdoor spaces contain no trees, grass or live plant materials of any kind. Sometimes it will be easy to add these materials, but in cases where the entire surface is filled with concrete, for example, it will be more difficult. It's not impossible, however, to help a space with this challenge become a place filled with nature; it just takes a bit more creativity. As mentioned earlier, adding planters (especially ones made from wood) filled with native grasses, flowering plants or small trees can help tremendously. Installing a greenhouse would also be an ideal way to bring daily contact with nature into children's outdoor time. Even removing a segment of concrete and planting grass and a tree can meaningfully change your space and provide children with daily interactions with nature.

IDEA: In spaces that are mostly covered with hard surfaces, even planting one tree gives children a way to interact with nature. In the photo above, children are mimicking the shape of this tree with their bodies.

IDEA: In spaces with little existing vegetation, plant trees, flowers and herbs in container gardens, wooden planters or clay pots to provide opportunities for children to interact with the scents, colors and textures of nature.

IDEA: Add a splash of extra color, if needed, by choosing bright planters such as those in the photo above.

Lack of Resources and Less-Than-Ideal Equipment

Lack of funds do not have to keep you from creating a wonderful outdoor space that encourages children to learn with nature. The good news is that nature provides a variety of free or low-cost materials that children love. For example, dirt makes a wonderful "canvas" for writing or drawing; pine cones, rocks or leaves are beautiful for creating mosaics; and willow branches work well as building materials. In addition, recycled materials such as large boxes from appliance stores can be used as temporary "loose parts" for children to enjoy. Lumber yards are often a good source for free pieces of wood or interesting rocks.

Many programs desiring to add more natural materials will need to work around already existing equipment that may be less than ideal. If equipment is unsafe, it will obviously need to be removed. Other existing equipment can be incorporated into a new plan for creating areas throughout the space. For example, an existing commercial climbing structure can be combined with a wooden balance beam and a crawl-through log to make a climbing and crawling area. Sometimes less is more. The judicial removal of less-than-ideal equipment might make room for more desirable spaces such as an open area or garden or "messy materials" area. Less plastic leaves more room for natural materials and creative play.

IDEA: **Climbing structures** don't always have to be manufactured. In the photo above, children are enjoying a natural climbing structure provided by a sturdy low branch from a wonderful old tree.

IDEA: **Use the free or low-cost materials that nature provides,** such as willow branches for building (above) or rocks, leaves, and feathers for mosaic-making (below).

IDEA: **Provide low-cost magnifying glasses,** as in the photo on the left, that encourage children to strengthen observation skills and delight in the beauty of nature.

Become a Certified Nature Explore™ Classroom

The Nature Explore Classroom Certification Program is a national initiative that recognizes schools and other organizations that have made a commitment to providing outdoor classrooms and comprehensive programming to help children use the natural world as an integral part of learning. Grounded in over a decade of research and field-testing, this widespread initiative is sponsored by the Arbor Day Foundation and Dimensions Foundation in collaboration with environmental, educational, design and health organizations. This program is open to any organization able to meet the following yearly requirements:

1. Well-designed outdoor space: Provide evidence that principles from the *Learning with Nature Idea Book* were used in the design of new spaces, or the redesign of existing spaces. For renewal, provide evidence of annual maintenance.

2. Staff development: Provide evidence that staff have attended a full-length Nature Explore Workshop. For renewal, provide evidence of annual professional development relating to nature education.

3. Family involvement: Provide evidence that activities or materials designed to increase family awareness and involvement in nature education for young children are provided regularly.

> "Children's conversations are much richer than they used to be. It seems like years ago we used to talk mostly about what they saw on T.V., but now, because of their experiences in the outdoor classroom, they have so many more things to talk about and to describe to us...and it's important."
>
> *Teacher Tami Britton, from a focus group interview*

Why Become a Certified Nature Explore Classroom?

You become part of a growing network of schools and organizations working to reconnect children with nature. Once certified you will be given your own page on a specially designated Nature Explore Classroom Web site which will also offer access to the latest news and research on children and nature, and encourage sharing of ideas.

When your outdoor classroom becomes certified, the Dimensions Foundation and the Arbor Day Foundation will send a press release to your local media to help you gain additional community recognition and support. Once certified, you will receive a Nature Explore Classroom sign, which you can post to publicly recognize your commitment, and to encourage others to create similar spaces in their own programs.

For more information on the program, or to request an application, go to arborday.org/certify or call 1-888-908-8733. Applications can be downloaded and submitted with documentation that the standards have been met.

References

Carson, R. (1965). *The sense of wonder*. New York : Harper & Row.

Cohen, S., & Horm-Wingerd, D. (1993). Children and environment: Ecological awareness among preschool children. *Environment and Behavior*, 25(1), 103-120.

Crain, W. (2001). How nature helps children develop. *Montessori Life*, Summer, 2001.

Hoffert, S., & Sandberg, J. (2000). Changes in American children's time 1981-1997. Center for the Ethnography of Everyday Life. Accessed June 1, 2004 from ceel.psc.isr. unich.edu/pubs

Kahn, P., & Kellert, S. (2002). *Children and nature: Psychological, sociocultural, and evolutionary investigations.* Cambridge, MA: The MIT Press.

Kelling, G., & Coles, C. (1996). *Fixing broken windows: Restoring order and reducing crime in our communities.* New York: Touchstone.

Louv, R. (2005). *Last child in the woods: Saving our children from nature-deficit disorder.* New York: Workman Publishing

Miller, D.L. (2007). The seeds of learning: Young children develop important skills through their gardening experiences at a Midwestern early education program. *Applied Environmental Education and Communication*, 6(2).

Moore, R. C., & Wong, H. H. (1997). *Natural learning: Creating environments for rediscovering nature's way of teaching.* Berkeley, CA: MIG Communications.

Nabhan, G., & Trimble, S. (1994). *The geography of childhood: Why children need wild places.* Boston: Beacon Press.

Pothukuchi, K. (2004). Hortiliza: A youth "nutrition garden" in Southwest Detroit. *Children, Youth and Environments*, 14(2), 124-155.

Rivkin, M. (1990). *The great outdoors: Restoring children's rights to play outside.* Washington, D.C: NAEYC.

Simmons, D. A. (1994). Urban children's preferences for nature: Lessons from environmental education. *Children's Environments Quarterly*, 11(3): 194-203.

Sobel, D. (1996). *Beyond ecophobia: Reclaiming the heart in nature education.* Great Barrington, MA: The Orion Society.

Taylor, A., Kuo, F., & Sullivan, W. (2001). Coping with ADD: The surprising connection to green play settings. *Environment and Behavior*, 33(1), 54-77.

Vygotsky, L. (1962). *Thought and language.* Cambridge, MA: MIT Press

White, R. (2004). Young children's relationship with nature: Its importance to children's development and the earth's future. Accessed June 11, 2004 from whitehutchinson.com/children/articles/childrennature.shtml

Wilson, R. (1994). Enhancing the outdoor learning environment of preschool programmes. *Environmental Education*, 46: 26-27 EJ484 153.

Wilson, R. (1997). The wonders of nature: Honoring children's ways of knowing. *Early Childhood News*, 6(19).

Following is a sampling of resources that will help you in your design or redesign efforts. This list is not meant to be comprehensive, but simply highlights a few good places to get started.

For more information on the Nature Explore program:

Arbor Day Foundation
www.arborday.org/explore
Dimensions Educational Research Foundation
www.dimensionsfoundation.org
Look for information on Nature Explore Classroom design consultations and certification; the Nature Explore Sourcebook for natural outdoor materials; workshops for educators and designers; Dimensions' research and other resources.

A sampling of organizations that care about nature education:

International Play Association   www.ipaworld.org
Look for information on promoting a child's right to play.

Keep America Beautiful, Inc.   www.kab.org
Look for regional nature connections.

Nature Action Collaborative for Children
www.worldforumfoundation.org/nature
Look for information on how to join this world-wide effort to make nature education a part of the lives of the world's children.

Nebraska Department of Education - Early Childhood
Training Center   http://ectc.nde.ne.gov/nature/nature.htm
Look for information, workshops, resource materials and practical strategies to connect young children with nature where they live, play, grow and learn.

North American Association for Environmental Education
www.naaee.org
Look for information about connecting children with nature.

Project Learning Tree   www.plt.org
Look for resources that encourage children to enjoy hands-on experiences with trees and nature.

Roots & Shoots   www.rootsandshoots.org
Look for classroom resources to help children see themselves as nurturing, caretaking individuals.

Resources to inspire interesting ideas:

Exchange Magazine
www.childcareexchange.com
Look for articles for educators, resources for parents, Beginnings Workshops and Out of the Box Training Kits focused on connecting children with nature.

National Audubon Society Sanctuaries and Nature Centers
www.audubon.org/local/sanctuary/
Look for a directory of Audubon nature centers that can support your efforts to connect children with nature.

The Outdoor Classroom Project, Child Educational Center, Caltech/JPL Community
outdoor-classroom@caltech.edu
Look for information on resources, educator workshops, seminars and center-site consulting on program and facility development.

Planet Earth Playscapes
www.earthplay.net
Look for creative and innovative ideas on outdoor space design.

Resources to help answer safety, accessibility, and design questions:

American Society of Landscape Architects (ASLA)
www.asla.org
Find landscape architects in your area.

The National Center on Accessibility
www.indiana.edu/~nca/
Look for information on making spaces accessible.

The National Program for Playground Safety
www.uni.edu/playground
Look for safety guidelines.

U.S. Consumer Product Safety Commission
www.cpsc.gov
Look for the *Handbook for Public Playground Safety*.

Acknowledgments

Primary Authors

Valerie Cuppens, Dimensions Educational Research Foundation
Nancy Rosenow, Dimensions Educational Research Foundation
James R. Wike, ASLA, RLA, Kersey/Wike Associates P.C.

Contributors

Sean Murphy, Being:Art
Eric Nelson, Outdoor Classroom Project
John Rosenow, The National Arbor Day Foundation
Anne Wike, RLA, Being:Art
Susan Wirth, The National Arbor Day Foundation

Reviewers

Linda Esterling, Early Childhood/Early Childhood Special Education Consultant
Dana Miller, Doane College, Dimensions Educational Research Foundatiion
Bonnie Neugebauer, Exchange Magazine, World Forum Foundation
Mary Beth Pistillo, The Nebraska Early Childhood Training Center
Michelle Rupiper, University of Nebraska-Lincoln
Janet Thompson, University of California-Davis

Special thanks to the teachers, staff and consultants at Dimensions Educational Research Foundation for their many invaluable contributions throughout the process of creating the content and design of this book.

Photography Credits

Key: T (top) M (middle) B (bottom) R (right) L (left)

Photographs © 2006 by: Being:Art, pp.13 TL, 34 BM, BR, 39 TR, BR, 47 TR, back cover TR; Peg Callaghan, p. 36 BR; Valerie Cuppens, pp. 4 T, 6 BR, 8 BL, 9 TL, 12 BL, 13 TM, MR, 15 BR insert, 19 M, 22 T, BL, 24 B, 25 TR, 28 T, 32 BL, 34 TR, 40 ML,41 BL, 42, 49 BR, 52, back cover ML; Brian Day, 50 M; fotolia, p. 19, 29 T, 31 BR; Theresa Frey, pp. 18 TL, 38 B; Suzan Haley, pp. 15 BL, 17 BR, 18 TR, BR, BL, 24 T, 41 TR, TM, back cover BL; Cindy Heinzman, p. 29 B; Geoff Johnson, front cover, pp. 2, 3, 7 TR, BR, 8 T, 10 BL, 11, 15 T, 17 BL, 31 TR, 39 T, back cover M, BR; Dana Miller, pp. 4 B, 6 BL, 12 T, BR, 14 B, 16, 17 TR, 20 TL, ML, TM, 21 BR, 27 BL, 29 M, BR, 30 B, 31 TR, 36 TR, MB, 40 T, 41 TL; Holly Murdoch, pp. 13 TR, 22 BR, 25 M, 32 MR, 39 BL, 40 BL, BM, 43 ML, MR, 48 M, BL, 51 R; Eric Nelson, pp. 32 BR, 33 BL, BR, 34 BL, 37 BR, 40 ML, M, 48 T; Beth Pauley, pp. 10 T, 14 M, 15 BR, 32 TR, 34 TL, 36 TM; photos.com, pp. 1, 9 TR, 28 B, 31 BL, 35, 36 TL, 37 T, 47 B, 50 LR, back cover; Leticia Roche Cano, p. 32 BR; Julie Rose, p. 40 BR; John Rosenow, pp. 9, 10 BR, 19 T, 20 BL, TR, 21 T, 23, 36 BL, 40 MR; Michelle Rupiper, p. 43 BR; Ann Watt, pp. 7 MR, 8 B; Donna Wheeler, p. 30 T; Joyce White, pp. 7 ML; James Wike, (sample plans) pp. 6, 44-46; Kerry Wilken, p. 14 TL; Susan Wirth, pp. 7 BL, 26, 27 T, 37 BL.

Photos were taken at the following locations: Arbor Day Farm Nature Explore Classroom, Nebraska City, NE; Brookfield Zoo, Chicago, IL; California Hospital Medical Center Child Development Center, Los Angeles, CA; Child Educational Center, La Canada, CA; Dimensions Early Education Programs, Lincoln, NE; The Downtown School, Memphis, TN; Hacienda Tabi, Yucatan Penninsula, MX; Hutchison School for Girls, Memphis, TN; Loyola Marymount University, Los Angeles, CA; Memphis Botanic Gardens, Memphis, TN; Ruth Staples Child Development Laboratory, University of Nebraska-Lincoln, Lincoln, NE; St. Peter's Early Childhood Development Center, Katy, TX.

RECYCLED PAPER RECYCLABLE / PRINTED WITH SOY INK